ASSERT
Yourself!

ASSERT
Yourself!

*Developing Power-Packed Communication
Skills to Make Your Points Clearly,
Confidently, and Persuasively*

Lisa Contini

**SkillPath Publications
Mission, KS**

Project Editor: Kelly Scanlon

Editor: Jane Doyle Guthrie

Page Layout: Premila Malik Borchardt and Rod Hankins

Cover Design: Rod Hankins

Library of Congress Card Catalog Number: 95-71732

ISBN: 1-878542-84-2

22   06 07 08 09 10 11

Printed in the United States of America

Contents

Introduction

Today's business world is hectic and fast-paced. You may have someone's attention for only a brief moment during a quick meeting, so you have to make your point clearly and emphatically. The current business climate is also competitive. If you want to be promoted or get your ideas implemented, you must make yourself heard above everyone else who has the same goals.

This new way of communicating demands a new set of skills. You can no longer rely on the "old school" of communication to lead you to success any more than you can rely on "old" technology to compete in today's marketplace.

These new skills may require you to abandon old but comfortable styles of thinking and interacting. For example, it used to be that employees listened to what the boss said and then did whatever they were told. In today's world, where traditional hierarchies are being replaced by "flat" organizations, void of the multiple layers of management you may know so well, there may be *no boss* to tell you what to do.

As a result, if you've always relied on your ability to carry out someone else's orders, you may be challenged to create your own path. And if you've always expected others to carry out your orders, you may be challenged to find another way to get the job done. All of this points to a new "technology" for communicating, one that relies on collaboration, not competition. A style of communicating that focuses on problems and solutions, not people and personalities. This new technology for communicating is called *assertive communication.*

Being assertive means communicating positively and with conviction; it is the ability to get your message across so that it's heard and recognized. Being assertive means asking for what you want clearly, directly, and with confidence. Assertiveness is more than the words you use; it's how you use them, what your body and vocal tone are saying, and timing your communications in the most effective way possible.

Being assertive does not mean manipulating others, being pushy, or acting ruthless—there's enough of that in the world already. Being assertive means evaluating what you want, being aware of others' needs, and looking for solutions and actions that best accommodate everyone involved.

If your tendency is to allow the needs and wants of others to determine your outcomes in life, then in the long run you will find yourself angry and depressed. If, on the other hand, you steamroll your way through life in the belief that it's a "dog eat dog" world out there, you may find that victory is sweet and *lonely.* These styles of communicating have become obsolete.

The good news is that there is a third alternative. That's what this book is about.

With its straightforward techniques and interactive exercises, *Assert Yourself!* will teach you how to evaluate your own level of assertiveness. You will begin by identifying what contributes to your ability to assert yourself, why it's easier sometimes than others to assert yourself, and how you can become an assertive, powerful person in all areas of your life.

Who you are on the outside is a direct reflection of what's going on inside. No matter how emphatic your words are, if you're feeling defeated and powerless on the inside, it's going to show. This book will teach you how to turn up the volume on the voice of possibility that lives in your head, to turn negative self-concepts into positive affirmations and become your own cheerleader.

With your head in the right place, you will find great success utilizing the models for assertive communication, whether it's asking for a raise, telling a co-worker how you *really* feel about a particular behavior, or getting your point across in a meeting.

How often do you find yourself caught off guard by an unexpected put-down or challenging statement? Don't you wish you could be ready with the perfect comeback, one that would leave you feeling confident, composed, and assured without being rude or hurtful, passive or defeated? Well, now you will be! This book will prepare you not only to survive but to thrive on the verbal battlefield.

Assert Yourself! contains what you've been looking for to help put forth the best of who you are with confidence and finesse. The practical information and interactive exercises you'll find here will get you ready to handle anything that comes your way!

Chapter 1

Three Styles
of Communicating

Being strong in no way implies being powerful, manipulative, or even forceful. By operating from strength, I mean leading your life from the twin positions of *worth* and *effectiveness*.

—Dr. Wayne W. Dyer

How do you respond when:

- It's 4:45 and a co-worker is standing over you, giving you an earful of gossip, when you have a report to finish and plans to meet with a friend right after work?

- Your manager volunteers YOU to do the research on a new project and you already feel "maxed-out" by your current workload?

- A co-worker uses racial slurs in describing a customer he's just had a problem with?

Do you internalize your feelings? Do you act on your anger and explode? Your reaction to such circumstances can reflect your level of assertiveness, and more important, influence the outcome of the situation. Generally speaking, you have three choices in communicating your reactions (or your overtures, in situations where you take the lead):

- Passive

- Aggressive

- Assertive

Asking yourself what is the *right* thing to do puts you in a position of judgment, measuring yourself against others. Am I as deserving and capable as this other person, or am I better and more deserving?

Judgment breeds conflict, both internally and with others; that's the significant distinction between aggressive or passive communication styles and one that's assertive. Assertive communicators don't see themselves as better than or less than others, but as equal to, both worthy and capable of handling a situation to best suit the needs of all involved.

Let's dig a little deeper into each of these three communication styles.

The Passive Communicator

The mental predisposition to a passive communication style causes you to nag yourself with the following sorts of questions (often not even consciously):

- How can I respond without hurting their feelings?

- Why do these things always happen to me?

- What do I need to say in order to have them like me?

Passive communicating is characterized by a "doormat" mentality. That is, you assume that others are smarter, better, and more capable than you are. Your responses to situations and stresses are reactive as opposed to proactive. Passive communicators also are notable for their silence and inward focus in the face of conflict, emanating a message of "It's my fault or it's not my fault, but I'm not capable of standing up for myself." Always offering profuse apologies, swinging between wishy-washy attitudes, turning the other cheek, constantly giving in—sound like anyone you know?

The outcome of passive communication is lose/win, with you on the losing side. If you choose the passive road over and over, hoping that someday someone will see you as noble and humble, you're in for a long wait. Most likely you'll find yourself walking away feeling victimized and later resentful of the people and situations you encounter.

The Aggressive Communicator

On the opposite end of the assertiveness spectrum is the aggressive response. The mental predisposition for an aggressive communication style has you fulminating inside over the following kinds of questions:

- Who do they think they are?

- Why should I sit here and take this?

- What can I say to put them in their place and keep them there?

Aggressive communicating is characterized by a "pit bull" mind-set. The focus here is almost exclusively outward, directed toward other people and often on fixing blame for problems. Aggressive communicators are combative and warlike, battering those around them with the message that "It's your fault and I'll tell you why!" Blaming, hurling accusations, always seeming righteous and indignant—does this sound familiar?

Though it may surprise you to hear it, passivity and aggression are both reactive, victim-like responses. Coming on too strong and shrinking from situations are each outward reflections of inner turmoil and insecurities.

The Assertive Communicator

Rather than looking for the *right* answer when faced with the need to respond, ask yourself the following significant questions:

- What do I want out of this situation?

- What do I think they want?

- What action/communication will yield the outcome I am looking for and preserve the dignity of everyone involved?

Your answers will prepare you to communicate assertively and will help you create a more positive outcome both for the moment and over the long term.

An assertive style of communication is powerful and free of judgment. In this state of mind, you stay focused on actions and results. Because they remain confident, direct, and objective, assertive communicators maintain the best interests of all involved. There are no victims here.

Three steps are necessary in becoming an assertive communicator:

1. ***Building awareness.*** First you must become conscious of your current style of communicating and be honest about the results it is yielding.

2. ***Increasing knowledge.*** Next you must learn how your responses to the events in your life shape the outcome of those events. Along with this, you need to understand how to change your responses from aggressive or passive to assertive by applying specific methods of communicating.

3. ***Developing skill.*** Without the ability to put your knowledge into practice, the knowledge itself remains useless. Reduced stress and increased enjoyment in your professional and personal life will come only with continued practice of the tools and tips offered here.

Try the following exercise. It's designed to build your awareness of the way you habitually respond to challenging events in your life.

Exercise One

How Do You Respond to Challenging Events?

As you read through each situation, circle the response that's most familiar or comfortable to you. Although you may be tempted to circle the answer you *wish* was most comfortable, doing so will only distract you from your goal of becoming an assertive communicator. Above all, don't try to figure out the *right* answer—this isn't a test!

1. You ask your manager about your review, which is two months overdue. She says, "Nobody else has gotten theirs either."

   A. "Nobody else has been here as long as I have without a raise."

   B. "I don't want to be a pest—it's just that I thought I might have done something wrong."

   C. "In order for me to successfully support the goals of our department, I would like to set a time for us to review my progress and look at what else needs to be done. How soon can we do that?"

2. You are offering a solution to a problem in your department meeting and a co-worker cuts you off before you can finish.

   A. You pound your fist on the table, stare into the other person's eyes, and continue talking louder and faster.

   B. You stop talking, sit back in your chair, and allow the other person to take the conversation from there.

   C. You lean into the conversation and give a "one minute" hand signal to the other person. When you're finished, you ask for that person's input.

3. The person who answers the phone at your workplace consistently makes errors in taking phone numbers and messages.

   A. You circle the errors in the message and leave them on the receptionist's desk with a note that says "My dog takes better messages than this!"

   B. You apologize to your callers for the errors, telling them that the receptionist tries hard. You say nothing to the receptionist.

   C. You bring the errors to the attention of the receptionist and together devise a plan to eliminate the mistakes.

4. A customer asks you to waive a service charge, saying other people in your company do so all the time.

   A. "Well, obviously whoever did that was wrong. That's probably why they aren't here anymore."

   B. "Oh, OK. Well, I guess I can do it, buy I'm really not supposed to."

   C. "I'm sure whoever that was made the best decision for those circumstances. Based on this current situation, we'd be happy to service you immediately at our standard rate. Would you like a morning or afternoon appointment?"

5. The company you purchase office supplies from promised you a discount on your next bill to make up for a service error, but when you get the bill there is no discount.

   A. "I was promised a discount because of the LAST mistake you made. If you think I'm paying this, you're crazy!"

   B. "I think there may be a mistake here. Do you think you might be able to help me if it's not too much of a problem? Maybe it's not really a big deal."

   C. "Hi, I'm calling about an error on my bill. The discount we discussed didn't appear on the invoice. Why don't you just tell me what the adjustment should be and I'll cut a check immediately."

6. Your supervisor gives you a verbal OK to take off on Friday, but then on Thursday evening tells you the department is behind and you need to be there on Friday.

   A. (arms crossed high on your chest) "I have a problem with that. You told me I could have the time off. How come you never do this to any of the night crew? Why do I get punished just because I work days?"

   B. (looking down) "But I thought you said you didn't need me. Now I don't have a baby sitter. I don't know what to do!"

   C. (with sincerity) "It sounds like this is important. You know that I'm committed to making this department run, and I made important plans for tomorrow. Perhaps there is another resolution, like working late tonight or coming in over the weekend. What do you think?"

7. During a meeting, a co-worker takes credit for an idea you came up with.

   A. You say nothing, but you look for an opportunity to steal one of her ideas or make her look bad. You get mad—and even!

   B. You say nothing to anyone and spend the next several days depressed, yelling at yourself for being stupid and taken advantage of.

   C. You confront her. "When you portray my ideas to our manager as your own, I feel as though I can't trust you. I shared my ideas with you in confidence, and you broke that trust."

8. You're having lunch in the cafeteria with several people from your organization. When the name of your friend comes up, the people you're with make fun of him.

   A. You make fun of the people there and ask them how they like it.

   B. You smile and say nothing, giving the impression that you agree.

   C. You say, "I'm not comfortable having this conversation. Martin isn't here to defend himself, and besides I enjoy his enthusiasm even if he shows it differently than I do."

9. You've been promised a larger work space in your new office in order to be more effective in your new position. When you move in, though, you are told, "Sorry, it didn't work out the way we thought it would."

   A. You slam drawers and yell at people while you're moving in. Every time a change comes up, you sarcastically relate it to the broken promise.

   B. You shrug your shoulders and quietly brood over the decision.

   C. You acknowledge that changes are bound to happen in a move like this, and tell the responsible party that in order to effectively serve your customers and co-workers, you will need more space. You offer alternatives and are open to creative solutions.

10. In front of your entire department, an employee accuses you of lying and playing favorites.

   A. Fed up, you point at the person and yell, "I'm sick and tired of your attitude. If you have all the answers, why aren't you the manager?"

   B. Embarrassed, you try to defend yourself by explaining your actions.

   C. You acknowledge the comment without getting defensive. "Obviously you have some questions about my decision-making process. I'd be happy to answer them as soon as we're through with this meeting."

Analyzing Your Responses to Exercise #1

For each of the previous scenarios, the "A" response was aggressive, the "B" response was passive, and the "C" response was assertive. (You may have figured this out after the first few!) The purpose of this exercise was not to identify which scenario is passive, aggressive, or assertive, but to raise your awareness of how you would most likely respond.

For each "A" response you circled, ask yourself the following questions:

- What do I feel I need to prove?

- How do I want the other parties involved to "pay" for what has happened?

- What is the likely outcome based on my response?

- What do I stand to lose by this response?

For each of your "B" responses, ask yourself:

- What am I afraid of?

- What is the likely outcome based on my response?

- What do I stand to lose by this response?

For each "C" response, ask yourself:

- Why did I choose this response?

- What is the likely outcome, based on my response?

- What do I stand to gain by this response?

Chapter 2

The Wellsprings
of Assertiveness
and Confidence

Our responses to the happenings in our
everyday life are shaped by who and what
we think we are.

—Nathaniel Brandon

Picture yourself sitting in front of your boss, about to ask for a well-deserved and long overdue raise. What's the voice inside your head saying?

- "I hope I don't blow it."

- "Maybe I don't deserve this."

- "I wish she wouldn't intimidate me."

- "Perhaps this isn't a good time to talk to him about this."

How many times have you talked yourself out of asking for what you want, telling someone no, or having an important conversation? Perhaps you were afraid of the response you might get, or you didn't want to hurt someone's feelings, or you decided at the last minute it didn't really matter. If you're like most people, the thought of launching into a difficult conversation makes you nervous. Suddenly your palms are sweaty, your heart is pounding, and you tell yourself this isn't really that important—maybe you're making a big deal out of nothing. In the end, you say something you regret, or worse, you say nothing at all!

Fear of sounding ridiculous, saying the wrong thing, losing a job, or damaging a relationship will undermine your confidence and get in the way of asserting yourself, if you let it. The good news, though, is you can train yourself to work through the fear and transform the negative thoughts into messages that support asserting yourself with confidence and getting what you want.

Here are three tools that will help you tackle this transition:

- Relaxation
- Thought Stopping
- Hearing the Voice of Possibility

You'll examine them each in turn in the following sections.

Relaxation

When you're physically relaxed, it's easier to concentrate and stay focused, especially in anxiety-producing situations.

Deep, even breathing is the most underrated prescription for relaxation there is. The short, shallow breaths associated with tension and anxiety inhibit the flow of oxygen to your brain and cause you to feel lightheaded. The effect also distorts your thinking. Taking deep, full breaths will help to settle you down and calm your mind.

You can practice the following breathing exercise anywhere:

1. Sit or stand with your back straight and your arms relaxed at your sides. If possible, close your eyes; if you can't, choose a focal point straight ahead, such as a picture on the wall or a tree outside your window.

2. Inhale slowly and deeply through your nose. Hold it for a count of two to three seconds.

3. Exhale gently and slowly through your mouth and picture all of your stress and tension flowing out of your body.

Repeat this process three times and enjoy the positive effects. With each breath in, visualize yourself inhaling wisdom, peacefulness, and confidence. With each breath out, exhale self-doubt, anxiety, and tension.

Thought Stopping

As you've no doubt discovered, it's certainly not difficult to find someone who, no matter what the idea or question, will tell you why you shouldn't, can't, or don't have a right to assert yourself. And just in case there's no one else around, you probably have your own built-in voice of limitation.

This voice of limitation is the pessimist who lives inside you, the little bully who pops up right on cue to remind you what a disaster it was the last time you voiced your disagreement in a staff meeting, for instance. It's the voice that lives by Murphy's Law: If something can go wrong, it will. The voice of limitation sees the limits to every situation and raises your doubts and worries accordingly. As you'd probably deduce, this voice or emotional trigger is generally counterproductive to positive assertive behavior.

This voice may have been with you for so long that it has become transparent. That is, you may no longer even be aware of what it's saying before you react to its message—therein lies the danger. In order to turn off this transmitter of perpetual doubt, you must first turn up the volume on it, raise your awareness to what it's saying, and recognize how it's affecting your communications.

Without this awareness, you'll remain a captive of your own limiting thoughts. Try the brief exercise that follows to become more aware of the voice of limitation that may be operating within.

Exercise Two

Increasing Your Awareness of Limiting Thoughts

Complete the following statements in writing, allowing yourself to listen to the voice of limitation without question or hesitation. Write down whatever comes to mind (do not edit or argue with it):

• When I feel like I can't ask for what I want, it's because I believe...

_____

_____

_____

_____

_____

_____

• When I feel like I can't accomplish a goal, it's because I believe...

_____

_____

_____

_____

_____

_____

The answers you came up with in Exercise #2 aren't grounded in reality—they're simply *beliefs*. Beliefs are our own self-drawn truths based on the results of our past experiences.

Suppose the first boss you ever had made fun of an idea you presented in front of your peers. You may have vowed at that time never to put yourself in that position again. So, in order to avoid embarrassment, the next time you were about to voice your opinion, your voice of limitation jumped in to remind you how humiliating it was the last time you tried to speak up.

In reality, of course, the situation is not the same—the people are different, the idea is different, the circumstances leading to the conversation are different—but your mind reacts to it as if it's exactly the same. In the end, this limiting belief keeps you from following through on your assertive communications.

Now that you've identified your voice of limitation, it will be easy to recognize it when it creeps up on you. And when you see it for what it is, you can very effectively muzzle it through a technique called *thought stopping*.

Try this right now: Go somewhere private (or just find a spot where you won't feel inhibited and also won't disturb anyone) and mentally zero in on a limiting thought that's been lurking in your mind. Turn up the volume on that voice until it's crystal clear. Listen to the voice for five to ten seconds, and then shout "Stop!" You'll notice that the voice in your head *will* actually stop.

Repeat the process a few times to get a feel for it, and then try it without yelling "Stop" out loud. Instead, shout it in your head.

Interrupting negative thoughts is an essential step in transforming limiting self-talk into positive messages that will open your eyes to unlimited possibilities.

Hearing the Voice of Possibility

Once you've discovered how to shut down the voice of limitation, you must immediately tune into the other voice that lives in your head: the voice of possibility. This is the part of you that sees limitations as temporary obstacles that you can and will overcome.

You've probably had the volume turned down on this voice for so long that you've forgotten what it sounds like. A simple exercise can help you get reacquainted with this good friend and ally. Take a few minutes to complete Exercise #3.

Exercise Three
Tuning In to the Voice of Possibility

Bring to mind a past success. Perhaps it was something as simple as developing an invoice form or as important as finishing school. Then think about the times you've asked for what you wanted. Maybe you invited someone out on a date or requested a raise. No matter how it turned out, you believed in yourself enough to ask. With these experiences in mind, complete the following statements:

- When I feel like I can ask for what I want, it's because I believe I...

_____

_____

_____

_____

_____

_____

- When I feel like I can accomplish a goal, it's because I believe...

_____

_____

_____

_____

_____

_____

24   Assert Yourself!

Too often we spend time looking outside ourselves for security and confidence. The truth is, you have the best coach and your most loyal fan living right inside of you. It may be difficult to hear that voice of possibility at first, especially after listening to the voice of limitation for so long. To help train your mind to listen for positive messages, try writing some positive self-concepts on 3x5 cards and carrying them with you. Whenever you have a few minutes—standing in line or waiting on hold—pull out the cards and read them to yourself. When possible, read them out loud.

You'll find over time that when you're holding back from asserting yourself, you can quickly tune into the limiting messages, shout "Stop!" in your head, and immediately replace the limiting thoughts with encouraging messages. There are other steps you can take as well to reinforce these positive messages and, in turn, your growing confidence:

- Record your "voice of possibility" on a cassette tape and listen to it on the way to work or before you fall asleep.

- Commit to practicing positive visualization by creating mental snapshots throughout the day. Simply close your eyes for five to ten seconds before you get on the telephone or walk into a meeting. Picture yourself communicating with confidence and assertiveness.

- Take five minutes at the end of each day and make a written list of every positive assertive communication experience you had that day. Next time you try to talk yourself out of having an important communication, refer to your list for inspiration!

Chapter 3

Preparing to
Be Assertive

Right thinking about assertiveness is crucial.
Thoughts, beliefs, attitudes, and feelings set the
stage for behavior.

> —Robert Alberti and Michael Emmons,
> *Your Perfect Right*

How often do you walk away from a situation thinking, "If only I had said…"? Was it because you clammed up or because you blew up? In either case, a prevalent afterthought is, "I need to manage my mouth better." The truth is, though, as shown in the previous chapter, your mouth usually isn't the problem—it's your thoughts that can get in the way. Other obstacles to asserting yourself include poor timing and the wrong environment.

Being prepared to be assertive includes the following considerations:

- Engaging in mental preparation

- Creating a supportive environment

- Using good timing

Each of these components plays a critical role in laying the groundwork for effective communications.

Mental Preparation

When you're churning over an upsetting situation with someone, do you spend hours rehearsing what you'd *really* like to say to that person, only to find yourself speechless or scattered when you're face to face? If you continue to hold on to your anger, it grows inside until you explode, right? And very rarely does pent-up frustration explode into a coherent and meaningful message.

Spontaneous outbursts usually come across as defensive, blaming, and irrational, leaving things worse than when you started— which also explains why you're inclined to hold back the next time. The secret to managing your mouth is to start by managing your head. While of course there are times when you're caught by surprise, very often you do have time to prepare for your interactions.

Suppose, for instance, that a co-worker has a habit of challenging your ideas in front of your peers, demanding that you justify your position on the spot. When this happens, you feel pressed to respond, but because you're preoccupied or not prepared for this challenge, you end up looking bad and apparently unable to present your ideas clearly. You leave the meeting angry and frustrated that once again this person has gotten his or her way at the expense of others (namely *you*).

After several of these incidents, you finally blow up. "Well, what do you want me to say? It doesn't really seem to matter what I think—the only thing you care about is getting your way!"

How do you suppose this looks to your peers and manager? Like a childish overreaction to a simple request for your ideas. That's what happens when you allow incidents like these to go on over and over without addressing them: you're the one who loses.

In this example, the assertive reaction would be a direct and private conversation between you and the troublesome co-worker to address the actions and results, not the people and problems. To do this, however, you must begin by getting your thoughts in order.

To prepare for the conversation, you must identify the following:

- Short- and long-term goals for the conversation

- Your assumptions

- The behavior you're having a problem with (rather than the personality trait)

- What you want from the person

- Why the person would benefit from changing the behavior

In the next chapter, you'll learn how to verbalize your thoughts; for now, the job at hand is organizing them. Let's start this process with an exercise. As you read through the steps on the next few pages, you can apply them to your own personal situatuon in the space provided on pages 33 to 36.

Begin by thinking of a situation that's been sapping your mental energy, one that involves a specific person whose behavior you'd like to see changed. Perhaps you feel taken advantage of by a co-worker, and you want that person to know you'll no longer do his or her work, that you feel ignored in meetings, or that you're being asked to do things outside your realm of responsibility.

In each of these situations, you undoubtedly hold some assumptions about how the other person will react if you try to discuss the behavior. Have you already decided that this co-worker will laugh it off if you bring up the issue? Do you *know* that people really don't care about what you say in meetings?

Thoughts like these keep you from asserting yourself, and if you're not aware of how these assumptions block your way, you become the victim of your own making.

The following steps are designed to help you separate assumptions from reality, allowing you to focus on the outcome and mentally prepare to be assertive.

Consider the following in regard to your situation:

- What you want to accomplish immediately/your short-term goal

  Example: "I want my boss to know that my education is important to me. I want to set boundaries on what I will do in overtime and on extra projects."

- What you want to accomplish in the long-term

  Example: "I want a mutually respectful relationship between me and my boss, to feel secure in offering my ideas and verbalizing my concerns. I want to be considered for a promotion to division manager."

- Your thoughts and assumptions about the other party involved and what the outcome will be

  Example: "If I assert myself and ask for what I want, my boss will deny me because he knows he has more power than I do. My boss will tell me I have to be willing to do what it takes."

While reflecting on your responses, recognize that your thoughts and assumptions are based on past experiences, and while those things may have been true in the past, they could also exist as part of a self-fulfilling prophecy. If you allow your doubts and fears to get in the way, they will. You have two choices: allow things to go on as usual and accept the consequences of your behavior, or try a new behavior and open up the possibility for a new response.

Next, consider some of the behaviors or actions of the person you're having trouble with. Be careful, though, to distinguish between actual behaviors and your judgments or the interpretations you assign them. For example:

Behavior	*Interpretation*
Rolls eyes when I am talking	Acts childish when I am talking
Is 15 minutes late to meetings	Has no respect for others' time
Interrupts when I am training	Acts like a know-it-all during training

When you observe a specific behavior, your mind decides right away what it means. This is your *interpretation*. What do you interpret or what do you think of when you witness the behavior you considered above?

The feelings you have regarding this situation—anger, concern, embarrassment, sadness—stem not from the other person's behavior, but from your interpretation of it. The behavior is just that, behavior. Think about it. Is it possible to see a co-worker on the telephone and feel fine about it? Of course it is. Is it also possible to see a co-worker talking on the phone and become enraged? *Yes.* Same action, different feeling-response, based on how you interpret the behavior.

Taking responsibility for and assertively expressing your feelings is always appropriate. Be prepared to do so by identifying your feelings about the situation. Now write the feelings you experience in the situation you've described.

You may be great at telling people what you don't like about their behavior, but don't forget to ask for what you want from them as well. Preparing to be assertive includes knowing what you want from the person—a specific action to replace the one that you don't like. For example:

Current behavior	New behavior
Rolls her eyes when I talk	Looks at me directly while I talk
Arrives fifteen minutes late to staff meetings	Arrives five minutes before the meeting starts
Asks at the last minute if I will stay late	Asks before 11 a.m. if I'll stay late

In thinking about what you want from the person or situation, you must define it beyond feelings like "respect," or vague requests like "equal treatment." If you truly want to improve the situation, you must not leave anything up to interpretation by the other person; his or her definition of respect may seriously differ from yours.

Finally, remember that the formula for assertive behavior is based on creating win/win agreements. Be prepared to point out how both you and others will benefit from the changes made. Describe the compensations; that is, what's in it for them to make a change? What are the benefits to you and to them? Sample benefits could include peace of mind, trust, saving time or money, security, and knowing what can be expected of you as well as what you can expect of others.

Having completed the steps in this process, you'll be mentally prepared to assert yourself by focusing on actions and results and taking responsibility for your feelings. In the next chapter, you will learn how to take your awareness and verbalize it assertively.

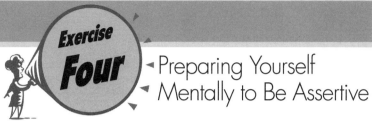

Exercise **Four** ◄ Preparing Yourself
◄ Mentally to Be Assertive

1. Write a brief description of a personal situation involving
   someone whose behavior you'd like to address.

   _____

   _____

   _____

   _____

   _____

2. Consider what you want to accomplish.

   A. What is your immediate or short-term goal?

   _____

   _____

   _____

   _____

   _____

   B. What is your long-term goal?

   _____

   _____

   _____

   _____

   _____

3. What are your thoughts and assumptions about the other person and about the outcome of a conversation with that person?

_____

_____

_____

_____

_____

_____

_____

_____

_____

4. What are some of the behaviors or actions of the person you're having trouble with?

_____

_____

_____

_____

_____

_____

_____

_____

_____

5. How do you interpret those behaviors/actions?

_____

_____

_____

_____

_____

_____

_____

6. How do you feel when you see the behavior you described in #4?

_____

_____

_____

_____

_____

_____

7. What would you like the person to do instead? Remember to be specific about this new behavior.

_____

_____

_____

_____

_____

_____

8. How will the other person benefit from making the change?

_____

_____

_____

_____

_____

_____

_____

9. How will you benefit from the other person's change in behavior?

_____

_____

_____

_____

_____

_____

_____

Creating a Supportive Environment

Preparing to be assertive also means choosing a physical environment that will support you. Factors such as the presence of others, personal space, and physical proximity will either add to your assertive interaction or sabotage it. Consider the following "do's" and "don'ts" of environment:

Do:

- Choose a neutral site such as a coffee shop or conference room.

- Speak with the person privately if the matter is private.

- Arrange a time when you have the person's undivided attention.

Don't:

- Risk embarrassing others in front of their peers.

- Sit and allow the other person to stand over you and look down on you.

- Continue an important conversation if the other person is preoccupied with paperwork or is transfixed by the television.

- Sit with a desk between you and the other person unless you want to be aggressive.

- Interrupt someone and demand to talk now.

Timing

What if you're still stewing over something that occurred some time ago—is it too late to be assertive now? While it's best to handle things as they occur, it's never too late to assertively address a situation that will benefit you and the other party. Keep the following in mind:

- Separate the past event rather than lumping it together with a bundle of incidents; the latter approach is likely to come across as aggressive ("And another thing, you ate my paste in kindergarten..."). When you respond to the straw that breaks the camel's back, the conversation is rarely productive.

- Start by letting the person know that this is an old issue. "I've been concerned about this for some time now" or, "While this happened a few weeks ago, I still think about it often."

- Consciously evaluate what's going on for the other person personally and professionally before you decide on the "right time" to talk. If your customer service representative is focused on a "hot" order you gave her, it's probably not the best time to discuss your concern with her billing system. When you rush into a conversation, you may lose in the end because the other person involved is not prepared to respond. Remember, being assertive means being committed to a win/win solution!

Chapter 4

Giving and
Receiving Feedback

No one can make you feel inferior
without your consent.

—Eleanor Roosevelt

A salesperson is meeting with a customer he's been doing business with for a long time. The purpose of the meeting is to renew their contract. During the conversation, the customer says: "Did I tell you I got a proposal from your competitor, the ABC Company? You should see their new pricing structure!"

If you were the salesperson, what decisions would you make from this feedback regarding your competition? If you're like most people, you would assume the prices ABC is offering are lower than yours, that your customer is going to ask you to match those prices, and that you have a long, tough negotiation ahead of you.

Are there other possible meanings behind this feedback? Of course there are. Perhaps ABC's prices are higher than yours, perhaps the pricing structure is complicated or doesn't make sense. While the tone of your customer's voice may add meaning to the statement, doesn't sarcasm sometimes sound the same as surprise or disagreement?

Human beings are feedback machines. We're constantly giving out information and responding to what's coming in. Some of this information is direct and constructive; at other times, it arrives in the form of nonverbal cues such as rolling eyes or off-handed remarks made under the breath.

Assertive communicators are direct in both giving and responding to information. They can and do separate their own feelings and assumptions from the messages they send and receive. Most important, they've learned to apply powerful feedback, a key strategy in responding with confidence to others.

Giving Powerful Feedback

In the previous chapter, you learned to prepare for being assertive by putting your thoughts on paper and separating your thoughts and beliefs from your feelings. The next move is to communicate your thoughts and feelings calmly and directly, without blaming others.

Four steps constitute powerful feedback:

1. **Specify the action or behavior you want to address.**

   "When I'm interrupted while I'm on the phone, … "

   Don't offer your interpretation and assumptions as fact. For example, don't say, "You obviously don't care about what I have to say." This aggressive statement will most likely trigger a defensive and combative response because of the implied accusation.

2. **Relate the feelings you experience as a result of the behavior.**

   "It's very frustrating for me … "

   You may think that if you tell others how you feel, they will label you as too emotional. Women, particularly, struggle with emotions in the workplace. However, emotions aren't the problem; what you *do* with them and how you *communicate* them is the problem.

   When you attempt to make someone else responsible for your feelings, that person's reaction will likely be to deflect the responsibility by putting the onus back on you. For example, if you say something like "You're always making me feel bad about my work," you almost guarantee a response like "You need to learn how to take constructive criticism." Blurting out "You embarrassed me in front of everyone in that meeting today!" may simply provoke an unsympathetic "Can't you take a joke?"

Instead, take responsibility for how you feel: "When you say things like that, I feel bad about the quality of my work," or "I'm not comfortable with personal comments such as the one you made in the meeting today." When you take responsibility and someone tries to deflect your comment by saying, "Well I can't help how you feel," you can then volley with, "Yes, my feelings aren't your responsibility, and I understand that it may not have been your intention to make me feel that way," or "That's right, my feelings are my responsibility, and that's why I'm taking the initiative to talk with you about this."

3. Describe the impact of the person's behavior.

"When my attention is divided, neither person is getting 100 percent from me, and that can lead to misunderstandings and mistakes."

When describing the impact of someone's behavior, be specific and concrete, pointing out the practical results of the person's actions. For example: "It's frustrating for me when the meeting is postponed to accommodate your tardiness, because the meetings then go overtime or are rushed. When we rush, productivity is lost, and when the meetings run overtime, our customers end up having to wait."

An aggressive response (such as accusing the latecomer of being selfish) would cause a debate over the person's integrity, and a passive response ("I know your schedule is really busy, but do you think you might be able to get here a little earlier next time?") will usually produce a perfunctory apology and no change in behavior.

4. Offer a solution that benefits everyone involved.

"If you need something from me when I'm on the phone, I would prefer that you hand me a note or wait until I'm finished. That way you know you have my undivided attention, and in the long run we'll all save time by avoiding misunderstandings."

Having verbalized the impact of a behavior, don't assume people will do anything differently unless you specifically ask them to. One of the biggest mistakes people make in this sort of communication is truncating the process at this point. You feel you've done a good job of separating your feelings and assumptions, and you've pointed out the impact of the behavior without accusing anyone of anything, so surely you don't have to spell it out, right? WRONG. Never leave it to chance at this point. You must assertively ask for what you want by offering a possible solution.

In the above examples of assertive communication, the speaker strategizes for success by focusing on actions and results rather than on people and problems, by taking responsibility for his or her feelings rather than blaming the other person for "frustrating me," and by offering a solution and directly addressing how the change in behavior would benefit the other person.

As an exercise to reinforce these four steps for yourself, bring out your mental preparation notes from Exercise #4. With these, you can create a conversational guide for an assertive feedback session. Referring to your notes, notice that you've already thought out most of what you want to say. You've already identified the behavior you have an issue with, your interpretation and feelings about it, what you want from the other person and the compensation or "what's in it for them" to change the problem behavior.

The following verbal equation will make it easy to take your thoughts and put them into words using the four steps to giving powerful feedback:

"When X (step 1), I feel Y (step 2) because Z (step 3). I would like A, because B (step 4). What do you think?"

To maintain powerful feedback, be direct and rational in your requests, and talk about what you *do* want, not what you don't want:

Ineffective:

"Don't ever look at me that way again!"

Effective:

"When I ask for your input and it's not a good time for you, tell me directly. That way, I don't have to try and decipher your nonverbal cues, and you know I will respect your request." Now, try applying the four steps yourself in Exercise #5.

Five ◄ Giving Powerful
◄ Feedback

Practice giving powerful feedback by building on the situation you addressed in Exercise #4.

Remember these four steps:

1. Specify the action or behavior.

2. Relate your feelings.

3. Describe the impact of the behavior.

4. Offer a mutually beneficial solution.

If you want, follow the verbal formula presented on page 44:

"When *X* (step 1), I feel *Y* (step 2) because *Z* (step 3). I would like *A,* because *B* (step 4). What do you think?"

Or, use your own structure. Just make sure the feedback includes all four steps and you specify what you *want*, not what you *don't* want.

Write your feedback here:

_____

_____

_____

_____

_____

_____

_____

Responding to Feedback

In many ways, giving powerful feedback is easier than responding to that of others. When you're the initiator of the conversation, you can prepare mentally and control the environment with much more ease than if you're caught off guard by someone else's remarks or demands. When a co-worker accuses you of trying to sabotage her, your boss rates you as less than satisfactory in a performance review, or an angry customer unloads his frustration on you, your natural and automatic response would be to either fight back (aggressive) or retreat (passive). It takes practice to remain neutral and respond assertively, with confidence.

As with giving feedback, responding to it entails both a mental exercise and a verbal one. What you say is a direct reflection of your assumptions and beliefs about the situation. An assertive response to feedback requires that you stay alert and focused, avoid taking the defensive, and exercise your voice of possibility.

There are four steps to responding assertively to feedback:

- Listen to what is being said.
- Acknowledge the message before responding to it.
- Ask clarifying questions if necessary.
- Offer a solution-oriented response.

1. Listen to what is being said.

When someone is talking, we often respond not to what is being said but to what we think the speaker means. The first and most critical step to responding to feedback is learning to listen, without judgment, to what is actually being said.

Listening is more than hearing something. Hearing is essentially an involuntary response; our brains automatically recognize sound entering our ears. Listening, however, is a selective process that includes what we see and how we feel, all of which influence our interpretation.

Being an assertive listener requires both *self-awareness* and *a desire to understand.* Self-awareness helps you consciously separate your own feelings and assumptions from that of the speaker. Further, through self-awareness, you pay better attention and stay present mentally. A common rule of contests and drawings is "Must be present to win." In the game of life, this holds true too. If you feel yourself thinking ahead, or focusing on the past, tell yourself to let it go and be present to what is happening *now.*

A desire to understand the speaker helps you control the natural impulse to read something into the speaker's message, thus avoiding adding fuel to the fire and making the situation worse. You must listen for the purpose of truly understanding how the world looks through the speaker's eyes. If you are listening for something to agree or disagree with, it may seem that you have only two choices—defense or surrender— which in turn can cause aggressive or passive behavior. You have another choice: to understand.

When you receive feedback, remember that it's only information, not The Truth. Someone providing feedback is simply describing his or her interpretation of your behavior, and that interpretation will include all sorts of information that has nothing to do with you: the person's childhood, the last company he worked for, how well she slept last night, and so on. Focus on understanding the feedback, not refuting it.

2. Acknowledge the message before responding to it.

People need to know they've been heard before they're willing to listen to you. Many people begin their response to feedback with a defensive explanation or counterattack message, which only signals victory to the speaker. A defensive response comes across as an admittance of guilt.

Funny enough, your reluctance to acknowledge the feedback because of the risk of appearing to agree with it is what causes you to appear "guilty as charged." Instead, demonstrate that you're listening without judgment by:

- *Breathing.* By consciously taking a deep breath before saying anything, you create enough of a pause to demonstrate that you're not on the defensive. Focus on inhaling through your mouth and exhaling through your mouth. This will help to keep you relaxed and alert.

- *Reflecting back what you heard.* Acknowledge the message by reflecting it back in your words without purposely changing its intent.

Notice the difference between the following two responses to feedback.

Boss: "I'm very angry about the way you handled this situation."

Employee Response #1: (purposely changing the intent of the message): "So, you think YOUR way is better, is that it?"

Employee Response #2: (correctly rephrasing): "You're not comfortable with the decision I made on this."

Notice in the second response that the speaker neither agreed nor disagreed, but rather reported on what he or she heard. In this scenario, the boss has nothing to fight back against. More important, if the boss agrees that your *interpretation* is accurate, you can calmly examine why he or she feels that way (keeping in mind that this is an interpretation of your behavior). Because you're not focused on agreeing or disagreeing, you will find it easier to remain assertive, focusing on the actions and results of the situation.

- *Finding truth in what the person is saying.* An optional additional technique in acknowledgment is to listen for and state the truth that you see in the feedback. Imagine yourself in the following situation:

    Co-worker: "You haven't been listening to a word I said. I guess now that you're a manager, you're too good to mingle with the worker bees."

    You: "You're right, I've been very distracted lately. I can see why you would feel the way you do."

    Notice that the first part of the response focuses on the action, not the tag on interpretation ("I guess now that you're a manager, you're too good to mingle with the worker bees").

    The second part of the response indicates neither agreement nor disagreement with the co-worker's assumption that you don't want to talk. Stay away from such an argument, because there is no way to win.

- *Apologizing, if appropriate.* One of the most difficult and yet most effective responses to feedback is to apologize for your action or its outcome. Once again, an apology is neither an admittance of guilt nor a passive surrender, if done correctly.

    You: "I apologize if I have offended you. What you have to say is important to me. If you would like to tell me again, I'd be happy to give you my undivided attention."

Notice the absence of excuses or explanations. Now read the following example, which is the same as the one above with an excuse added, and see how the excuse colors the response.

You: "I apologize if I have offended you. What you have to say is important to me. If you would like to tell me again, I'd be happy to give you my undivided attention. It's just that I have a lot of added responsibility now, and I won't always be able to listen to every little comment people want to make anymore."

3. Ask clarifying questions if necessary.

Clarifying questions are gentle probes that help you better understand the speaker's point of view or will uncover important information that will lead to a resolution. Take care, though; clarifying questions can be mistaken for challenges or justification, as in the following:

Co-worker: "I just don't feel like I'm getting the support I need on this project."

You (spoken with sincerity): "What specifically do you need that you aren't getting now?"

You (spoken with sarcasm): "What do you mean, *support?* What *else* do you need?"

In the second response, the speaker is clearly challenging the co-worker in the guise of a clarifying question. In the first, the speaker is asking a question to gain a clearer understanding of what the co-worker needs.

The feedback we receive is very often vague and, in some cases, accusatory. Asking clarifying questions will help you to pinpoint the behavior or specific action that the person giving the feedback is having a problem with.

In giving powerful feedback, you will recall, the first step is to isolate the behavior or action you have an issue with and separate it from your feelings and assumptions. When you're on the receiving end of feedback from people who don't have the same level of self-awareness that you now have, they will rely on their *interpretations* of your behavior and blurt out vague statements such as "You're not being the team player I need," or "You have no respect for me or this company," or "Why am I always the one who has to clean up after your messes?"

A good assertive communicator realizes that if he or she reacts to these emotional statements, the result will be disastrous. Before responding, it's wise to ask clarifying questions to isolate the actions and results that form the root of the issue. Assertive communicators who aren't sure of a speaker's meaning will ask questions such as the following:

"What do you mean by _____?"

"Do I understand correctly that... ?"

"I'm not sure I understand. Would you be more specific?"

"What is your understanding of... ?"

"What have you tried so far?"

"What do you think needs to be done at this point?"

"How does it appear to you?"

"What is it about my work that you would like to see changed?"

To familiarize yourself with this important process, try Exercise #6, "Asking Clarifying Questions."

Exercise Six — Asking Clarifying Questions

Create two additional clarifying questions in response to scenarios A and B below (noting that you must first acknowledge the person before asking clarifying questions; if you skip the acknowledgment step, your questions, no matter how gentle, will most likely be perceived as a challenge):

Scenario A

Receptionist: "This is the third call from your daughter today. I'm not your private secretary, you know."

You (acknowledging the feedback): "You have been very gracious about handling my personal calls. I know it's not a requirement of your position and it takes time away from your work."

Receptionist: "I'm just really tired of being expected to be everything to everyone."

You (clarifying):

1. "What sorts of things do you feel you are expected to do?"

2. _____
   _____
   _____

3. _____
   _____
   _____

Scenario B

Boss: "It seems to me that if you spent as much time on your work as you do socializing, you wouldn't have to stay late."

You (acknowledging the feedback): "It looks to you like a matter of time management, not workload."

Boss: "Well, yes. The last person in your job was never here past 5:15 or 5:30."

You (clarifying):

1. "From your perspective, how has the workload changed since I've been in this position?"

2. _____
   _____
   _____

3. _____
   _____
   _____

Review what you wrote and ask yourself: "Why am I asking this question? To gain understanding, or to build my case?"

4. Offer a solution-oriented response.

Once you have acknowledged the speaker and isolated the specific action or behavior of interest, it's time to "problem solve." Assertive solutions fulfill the needs of both parties, are specific and measurable, and are tied to actions and results. For example, instead of "Let's both beware of each other's needs more often," try "Let's meet every Monday morning and Friday afternoon to make sure both our needs are being met."

Arriving at a solution should be a collaborative process. Begin by asking solution-seeking questions such as:

"What do you feel would be an acceptable solution?"

"Where would you like to go from here?"

"Based on your past experience, what works best under these circumstances?"

By soliciting input from those who give you feedback, you're not suggesting that you have no input, or that you'll do whatever they ask; you're acknowledging that they're the ones having difficulty. (And most people like their own solutions best.)

Sometimes, however, the solution offered may be less than desirable. Here are some strategies for dealing with some of those situations:

- **The solution is not one you agree with.** For example, "I think you should give us the product for free. After all, you're the one who doubled the shipment by mistake."

  Here you might respond: "That's one option. What would some others be?" When people make outrageous requests, they're still operating from their emotions. The best thing is to acknowledge their response without judgment.

- **The solution is vague.** For example, "You just need to show more respect for others' ideas."

  An appropriate response here could go something like this: "It's important to me that others know I respect their ideas. It would help me if you'd give an example of what I can do to show my respect."

- **No solution is offered.** For example: "I don't know what to do. You're the boss—you tell me!"

  Direct the shared responsibility for problem solving back toward the speaker with a response such as: "That's right, I am. And I would never want to assume that what works for me would work for you. I'm here to ensure that you have the resources you need to handle these challenges. If you were the boss, what would you suggest?"

To gain practice at offering solution-oriented responses, try Exercise #7 on page 56.

In addition to the skills just described, there are a few other "rules of the road" for assertively responding to feedback:

1. Don't react. The best defense is *no* defense.

2. Don't interrupt the person giving you feedback except to request moving your conversation to a supportive environment.

3. Maintain eye contact. Looking down signals submission or lack of interest.

4. Don't cross your arms or legs; maintain an open, powerful stance.

5. Keep telling yourself: "This is only information. This is only information."

Armed with the right moves and the confidence to use them, you'll be a pro at giving and receiving feedback.

Exercise Seven ◀ Practicing Solution-Oriented Responses

Rewrite the solutions/responses listed below so that they are specific, measurable, and focused on actions and results.

1. "Treat everyone equally. Don't show favorites all the time."

_____

_____

_____

_____

_____

_____

2. "Don't be so pushy all the time."

_____

_____

_____

_____

_____

_____

3. "Stop gossiping so much and get to work."

_____

_____

_____

_____

_____

_____

_____

4. "Don't embarrass me anymore in meetings."

_____

_____

_____

_____

_____

_____

Chapter 5

Getting What
You Want

Decide what you want, decide what you
are willing to exchange for it. Establish
your priorities and go to work.

—H.L. Hunt

Do you have a hard time asking for what you want? Does it seem selfish to focus on your own needs? Maybe you're afraid that if you ask for help, you'll appear weak and incompetent, or possibly that people will accuse you of being too demanding.

Asking for help, or "The Art of Making a Powerful Request," is one of two important keys to your success in communicating assertively. Ever heard the saying, "If you don't ask, you don't get"? If you know how to ask for what you want, your life will be much easier, plus you'll be surprised how often you get what you want!

The second, absolutely crucial key to getting what you want is learning to say "no." Surprisingly, many people find it much harder to refuse someone else than to ask for something on their own behalf.

Making a Powerful Request

Before discussing how to effectively ask for what you want, let's take a look at what not to do:

- Don't beat around the bush.

    "I wish I had a little more time on this project... "

    "If only I didn't have to go to that meeting alone..."

    "I can hardly make ends meet on this salary... "

- Don't be apologetic.

    "I hate to ask you this... "

    "I know you really hate to, but could you maybe... "

    "I'm really sorry to bother you about this... "

- Don't make a statement instead of a request.

    "This needs to be handled."

    "I don't have time to do this myself."

    "The files are out of alphabetical order."

- Don't cast your request in the negative.

    "Never be late to this meeting again."

    "Stop treating me like I'm your child."

    "Quit using my computer without asking me first."

Now, here's what to do to format a powerful request:

- Be specific.

  "In order to move forward on this, I'll need your feedback by 2 p.m. Can you have it to me by then?"

- Offer a benefit.

  "I want to give this project the attention it deserves. In order to do that, I'd like thirty minutes of uninterrupted time. Will you please handle my calls for the next half hour?"

- Be positive rather than negative.

  "Please arrive at the office ten minutes before the scheduled meeting time. If you have a conflict, I would like to know twenty-four hours before the meeting."

Try your hand at Exercise #8 and practice making powerful requests. For ongoing practice, start paying particular attention to the requests you hear passing back and forth between co-workers or members of your family. Mentally critique or edit them using the guidelines discussed previously.

As a reinforcing exercise, rewrite the following statements into effective requests. The first item has been completed for you, but come up with your own response as well.

1. "I wish you wouldn't give me projects like this at the end of the day."

   Example: "In order for me to give these reports the attention they need, it's important that I have at least two hours' notice. How does that sound?"

   _____

   _____

   _____

   _____

2. "You are always late to our meetings."

   _____

   _____

   _____

   _____

3. "I really hate to ask you this, but do you think maybe I could leave early on Friday?"

   _____

   _____

   _____

Saying "No"

"No" is undoubtedly one of the first words you learned to speak, and you probably used it freely for the first years of your life. Then why is it so hard to say it as an adult? Take a few minutes to complete each of these statements:

> "If I say 'no,' I'm afraid... "
>
> "If I don't say 'no,' I'm afraid... "
>
> "It's OK to say 'no' when... "
>
> "It's not OK to say 'no' when... "

For many people saying "no" has an underlying meaning of "I don't like you" or "I don't care about you." Saying "no" often carries a burden of guilt or fear of challenging someone else's value system.

Suppose your best friend asks you to donate fifteen hours this weekend to a charity event. You, though, have been busy every weekend for the past two months and have been looking forward to an entire Saturday and Sunday of quiet time. You want to say "no," but you don't want to look insensitive, so you make up an excuse about a sick relative. Your friend still presses you. Finally, you give in. You feel trapped, manipulated, angry, maybe even resentful of your pushy friend for "making you" do something you don't want to do.

Sound familiar? Here's another way to look at this scenario. *You chose your actions.* By saying "yes" just to look good in the eyes of your friend, you said "Your values are more important than mine."

Most of us struggle with honoring our own values, choosing our actions in hopes of winning the praise and recognition of others, and them blaming them for the negative consequences of our actions. Suppose you work on the charity event, don't get enough rest, and then end up missing work the next week because you're sick. Whose fault is it that you didn't get enough rest? Yours, of course. "But how could I refuse a charity event?"

Just remember: *Every time you say "no" to someone or something, you are saying "yes" to someone or something else.*

Assertively saying "no" doesn't mean harshly cutting people off and barking refusals at requests because you don't "feel like it." Assertively saying "no" means being aware of and acting in alignment with your own values and goals. For example, if your supervisor asked you to be the "lookout" while several employees loaded thousands of dollars of company property into a stolen van, would you hesitate to refuse? Of course not, because saying "yes" would conflict strongly with your value of honesty. In this case, saying "no" to your supervisor would mean saying "yes" to integrity and trust.

Often, though, your choices may not be as clear to you as the blatant example above. For example, when you say "no" to staying late to work on a project, what are you saying "yes" to? Possibly your education, your family commitments, or your health. Saying "no" is not about uttering the word; it's about making tough decisions, being true to yourself, and considering the impact of your actions on those around you.

There are three steps to saying "no" and feeling good about it:

1. **Evaluate the outcome of the request against your values and goals.**

   The best check is to ask yourself these two questions:

   - "What do I stand to lose by saying 'no'?"
   - "If I say 'no' to this, what am I saying 'yes' to?"

For example, suppose you are asked to take on an extra project requiring an additional fifteen to twenty hours of work per week. What do you stand to lose by saying "no"?

- You may not be asked to work on future projects.
- You may be talked about negatively behind your back.
- You may be left out of decisions that impact your department in the future.

If you say "no" to this, what are you saying "yes" to?

- Your sanity.
- Getting home by 5:30 every night.
- Doing a thorough job on the projects you're in charge of now.
- Being available to support your staff on their projects.

2. **If your choice is "no," make a list of other options and resources available to accomplish the task.**

For example, suppose top management asks you to take on all the duties of the sales manager while she's on maternity leave. You can present several options in reply:

- Split the duties between several staff members.
- Choose one or two activities that you excel in and volunteer to do those.
- Recommend other staff members to help out in areas you're not interested in or don't feel comfortable doing.

Though actually refusing the request, you come across as a problem-solver and flexible thinker.

3. Don't say the word "no"; talk about what you will do.

It's all in the presentation. Keep the following "do's" and "don'ts" in mind when assertively saying "no":

Don't say...

> "I can't."

> "That's not my job."

> "What choice do I have?" (playing the martyr)

> "I'd like to, but... "

Do say:

> "Here's what I can do... "

> "The best person to help you with that would be... "

> "I understand your request, and here's my concern... What are some other alternatives?"

> "In order to maintain the level of excellence expected on this, I'd like to suggest the following options (from step 2)... "

To get in some practice in saying "no," try responding to the situations in Exercise #9.

As you engage in the verbal volley of making requests and deftly turning them down, you may begin to picture yourself in a tennis match of sorts. That physical analogy is a good one for more than the obvious reasons—there's also a physical dimension to assertive communication, called "nonverbal cues," which you'll explore in the next chapter.

Learning to Say "No" Assertively

How would you assertively say "no" to the following requests? The first item has been completed for you, but try writing your own response anyway.

1. "I really hate taking minutes at the meeting. Since you are much better at it than I am, would you do it for me, please?"

   Example: "To make sure we all participate in the meeting, why don't we rotate that responsibility? Who would like to volunteer for this week?"

   Your Response:

   _____

   _____

   _____

   _____

   _____

2. "We need your help. I know this isn't your job anymore, but no one else here seems to be able to get the system to work. Would you mind helping us out?"

   Your Response:

   _____

   _____

   _____

   _____

3. "I need this before you go home tonight. Just leave it in my desk if I've already gone."

   Your Response:

   _____

   _____

   _____

   _____

Chapter 6

Asserting Yourself
Nonverbally

Facial expression is human experience
rendered immediately visible.

—Edmund Carpenter

Who you are *physically* speaks louder than anything you say. Experts report that when you speak, 93 percent of your listener's interpretation has to do with everything *but* what you are saying. The listener makes decisions about the accuracy of the information, how trustworthy you are, and many other things based on the delivery of your message rather than on the content.

Just to see how this works, commit one week to studying the nonverbal communication habits of those around you. Watch the people you look up to and trust as well as those you don't think so highly of. Pay attention to how they walk and what they wear as well as to their posture, gestures, facial expression, and vocal tone. Turn on the television at home and turn off the sound. Observe how people communicate their feelings about themselves and others without uttering a word.

Being assertive verbally means very little unless your nonverbal communication supports your spoken message, and while you're learning, you can "fake it till you make it." That is, by practicing the skills that will be discussed here you can appear confident and assertive even if you don't feel that way. In fact, evidence supports the theory that the mind will respond to what the body does physically (try to smile and stay angry at the same time), so acting assertive physically can only help you feel assertive more readily.

Before exploring the specifics of nonverbal communication, it's important to note the following: Many nonverbal signals and cues do not mean the same in other cultures as they do in yours. The tips discussed throughout the rest of this chapter are based on what's generally expected and accepted in the American culture. If you work and live in a highly diverse cultural environment, you should actively seek to discover what the rules of those cultures are.

Eye Contact

"The eyes are the windows of the soul." It's true that your eyes can give away your true feelings without you even realizing it.

Look people directly in the eye when speaking to them. Rather than stare, though, glance away naturally from time to time to create a sense of comfort. Maintain eye contact especially when you feel intimidated or want to "run and hide."

In a one-on-one conversation, do anything you can to keep eye contact level with the other person. Any time one person stands and the other sits, it creates a subconscious division of power. If you're seated, ask the other person to take a seat. If the person refuses, then stand up.

When participating in a meeting, make consistent eye contact with the speaker. By doing so, you will send a message that says "I respect you, I am listening, and I am important too." Imagine earning the respect of the speaker without saying a word!

Ask a friend, relative, or co-worker to engage in the following
activity in order to raise your awareness of eye contact patterns
and to practice assertive eye contact. One of you will be partner
A and the other partner B.

1. Partner A, bring to mind an important matter in your life,
    something you feel strongly about. It may be a political
    issue, the performance or lack of performance of a co-
    worker, or a personal relationship you're struggling with.

2. Partner B, when A first starts talking, look him or her in
    the eye and nod occasionally. After a few moments,
    break eye contact by looking down or away, as if you're
    distracted by something else in the room or simply aren't
    interested. After another moment or two, reestablish eye
    contact. The whole process should take about sixty
    seconds. (It's best to do this with a timer, so you don't
    have to think about time. If you do the exercise in a
    group, the facilitator can act as the timekeeper.)

3. When the time is up, partner A should answer these
    questions:

    •   How did it feel when Partner B was making eye
        contact with you?

    •   What were you thinking when your partner looked
        away while you were talking?

    •   How did your partner's eye contact pattern affect
        how you trusted him or her?

Partner B should answer these questions:

- What did you notice about partner A's body language and vocal tone when you were maintaining eye contact versus when you were looking away?

- What did you notice about what you heard or how well you were listening when you were making eye contact versus not making eye contact?

4. Switch roles and repeat the entire exercise.

Distance and Spacing

"Personal space" refers to the comfortable distance two people maintain as they communicate. Personal space changes depending on the relationship you have with the person, gender differences, and the presence or absence of conflict.

Two people engaged in a friendly conversation will stand approximately an arm's length apart. Invading this space signals aggressiveness; increasing it signals submissiveness.

If you want to get someone's attention and physically assert yourself, you can step or even lean into his or her personal space for a moment or two. If you stay much longer than that, not only do you risk being labeled "pushy" or "bossy," you lose the attention of the person you're trying to talk to.

You also can demonstrate your assertiveness by standing your ground when you feel frightened or offended. Backing up is usually interpreted as backing down. Staying put and maintaining consistent eye contact in the face of conflict says more than any words could impart.

Exercise Eleven ◄ What a Difference Distance Makes

Ask a friend or business associate to participate in this exercise with you:

1. Begin by standing facing your partner. Stand the distance you would when having a friendly conversation. Notice how safe you feel standing this distance apart.

2. You and your partner should then take one step toward one another and stand there for a moment. Notice how it feels to decrease your personal space before returning to your beginning stance. If someone stands this close to you or leans into you like this while talking, what are the assumptions you make about that person?

3. Starting from the "friendly" distance, both you and your partner should next take one step back, away from one another. Stand there for a moment and notice how this feels. If someone kept this distance from you, what assumptions might you make about that person?

Posture and Gestures

Generally we give more credibility to those who take up more space. That is, body posture and gestures can create an illusion of either dominance or weakness.

Be aware of yourself over the next week. Notice whether your tendency is to "shrink" in the face of challenge or conflict. While crossed arms and legs, slumped shoulders, and a downcast head are typical of anyone who feels weak or defensive, these tendencies are more prominent in women. Given the fact that women are usually smaller than men in girth and stature, these automatic physical responses to uncomfortable situations can be even more damaging to women who wish to communicate assertively.

Stand up straight. A good way to practice is to stand up against the wall for several minutes so you can feel the back of your head, your shoulder blades, your hips, and your heels all pressed against the surface. Then take a short walk around your home or office, doing your best to maintain that posture. At the end of the walk, back up against the wall and see how well you did at holding yourself erect.

In addition to posture, gestures can add to or diminish your assertive demeanor. Gestures should be purposeful and outwardly sweeping. Women should avoid playing with hair and jewelry or keeping their hands folded and stationary for long periods of time. Hands on the hips and pointing fingers are power gestures for men, but come across as "mothering and nagging" when used by women. For a woman, power gestures include punching the air with closed fists or making a steeple with the index fingers while making a pointing gesture.

The Handshake

The most common form of touch in the workplace, a handshake tells someone from the moment you meet whether you are a doormat, a pit bull, or an assertive, confident peer. A handshake is as personal as your signature and worth practicing. A limp, cold handshake signals fear, apprehension, or aloofness. Someone who is a "finger crusher" may be overcompensating for a lack of self-confidence or attempting to intimidate.

An assertive handshake is firm without being painful. It is brief and accompanied by a smile and direct eye contact. Practice your handshake with a partner. Move your hand forward into your partner's palm until the fleshy part of your hand between thumb and forefinger meets your partner's. Firmly wrap your fingers around your partner's hand and give it one or two firm shakes.

Vocal Tone

Are you a mumbler? Do people refer to you as "soft-spoken," or are you often asked to "tone it down"? The volume and quality of your voice will enhance or take away from your level of assertiveness in terms of how others perceive you.

You be the judge! Take a small tape recorder to work with you, turn it on, and forget about it (to the extent that you can). Later, when you're alone (it's usually less embarrassing that way), listen to yourself. Try to disconnect the content from the quality of your voice. How would you label the confidence level of the person you hear?

Listen for speed—do you sound like you're late for a train, or are you talking so slowly you don't have time to listen to yourself? Most important, does your vocal quality match the intent of your message? If you giggle through a reprimand or serious message, or speak matter-of-factly about an important, exciting issue, this may be why people aren't taking you seriously.

If you want to improve the sound of your voice, audio programs such as *The Sound of Your Voice* and courses offered through most junior colleges will assist you in perfecting your vocal tone and quality.

Being aware of your nonverbal "language" and becoming adept at using it to your advantage will add a potent dimension to your overall communication package.

Chapter 7

Asserting Yourself
in a Meeting

In essence, every meeting you attend is a
prospective job interview and a current
job evaluation.

—George David Kieffer

With the emergence of Total Quality Management and self-directed work teams, more decisions are being made in meetings than ever before. Your lack of assertive communication skills in a meeting setting may pose an obstacle to your professional growth.

Whether you're the designated leader of the meeting or not, it is your responsibility as a participant to make the meeting productive. Your performance in a meeting says a great deal about your leadership style as well as your ability to make decisions and manage your workload.

Prepare Beforehand

A teacher once said to a student who didn't have a pencil for class, "Coming to school without a pencil is like going to swim class without your trunks!" In other words, be prepared! Familiarize yourself with the topic of the meeting, talk with other participants, or gather information from other sources if necessary.

It's all too common in today's workplace for people to come and go, answer telephones, and duck out of meetings to "grab a file." *But because it's common doesn't mean it's acceptable.* Your ideas will more likely be considered and your input taken seriously if you have demonstrated your commitment through preparation.

There are several steps you can take to arrive at a meeting prepared:

- Review the agenda and make notes on each item regarding questions or comments you may have.

- If you're unclear about the purpose of the meeting, ask the leader for clarification before things get started ("Margaret, in order to make the best use of our time in the budget meeting this afternoon, I'd like to confirm the specific purpose of the meeting. Will this be a brainstorming session, or is our goal to make final decisions?").

- Do your research. For example, if you would like to assert your ideas on how to make better use of the computer system, be prepared with documentation and specifics on how to make it happen.

- If you're presenting information in writing, always make sure it is "final draft" quality and have enough copies for every participant (plus extras, just in case). If you have to run out of the room to make more, you risk losing credibility.

During the Meeting

Leading or simply participating in a meeting can challenge your assertive communication skills in many ways. The following examples present some of the most common challenges.

Interruptions. You have a great idea, but every time you try to get it out of your mouth, someone interrupts you. If you allow yourself to be interrupted, you send a message that says, "Go ahead, I'm sure what you have to say is more important." The question is, how do you politely tell someone to "sit down and shut up"?

Actually, there's a progression of tactics to use when handling interruptions. Always start with number 1, but if it fails, move on to number 2 and so on.

1. Send nonverbal signals. Speak louder and deeper, hold up one hand to signal "stop," and continue talking.

2. If the interrupter continues, add a verbal cue ("I'm not finished yet, thank you") and continue talking. Address your comments to the whole group, using random eye contact with other participants and breaking eye contact with the interrupter to signal that you're not going to be distracted by the interruption.

3. If the interrupter insists, add the power of touch by placing one hand firmly on the person's arm. Look directly into his or her eyes, and say: "Please let me finish. (pause) Thank you." (If the person is not close enough to touch, leaning forward toward him or her to the point of being out of your seat will create a similar effect.) Make sure you pause for a moment once you have the person's attention, look him or her straight in the eye when you say "thank you," and immediately continue what you were saying, addressing the entire group with your gestures and eye contact.

Note: Once you've successfully captured the attention of the group, get to the point. Now is not the time to philosophize and divert from the matter at hand.

Someone is dominating the discussion. When a meeting participant (usually an energetic, gregarious one) has a comment or lengthy opinion about every item on the agenda, one of the worst outcomes is that it can shut down or silence others at the table. Reining in these dominant types requires an assertive, straightforward approach: Acknowledge their contribution, and then ask for the input of someone else by name. "Thank you, Bart, you obviously have put a lot of thought into the subject. Julie, what are your thoughts on the subject?"

Side conversations are going on. Side conversations are not only disruptive and distracting—they potentially withhold good ideas and useful observations from the group at large. When "sidebars" break out, regain the attention of the group and emphasize the benefit of sharing ideas with the whole group. "I'm glad to see that you all have ideas on this. Let's hear from you one at a time. Bill, I believe you were finishing a thought."

Someone comes in late. Whether occasional or habitual, latecomers must be dealt with at most meetings. Don't say, "That's all right"; it's not. If you stop your meeting to review for those who show up late, you risk losing control, breaking continuity, and angering participants who arrived on time. Simply acknowledge these people and ask them to be responsible for finding out what they missed.

An issue arises. For 99.999 percent of the times that someone brings up an item that's either not on the agenda or doesn't align with the purpose of the meeting, it's not appropriate or necessary to amend your agenda or lengthen the time of the meeting. Use the "parking lot" technique instead. List on a board or ask someone to take down any important items that need to be handled outside the meeting. If the issue persists, stop the meeting only long enough to schedule a separate time to handle the issue.

Your familiarity with complicated issues, your seniority or position in the company, your confidence with regard to your own ideas and abilities—all of these and many other variables can affect your desire and resolve to communicate assertively at meetings. But the techniques and insights in this chapter offer a strong springboard for your plunge into these very important business interactions.

Chapter 8

Dealing With
Difficult Personalities

Your hurts come not from what others do
to you, but from what you choose to do
with their actions.

—Dr. Wayne W. Dyer

Practicing your assertive communication skills with other
assertive personalities will be relatively easy; finding
yourself face to face with a bully or a back stabber will offer
the true test of your assertiveness repertoire.

Although everyone you'll interact with is unique, therefore
requiring you to adapt your communication techniques
accordingly, "difficult personalities" evidence certain
commonalties and in general respond to certain strategies on your
part. When possible, practice these tactics with a close friend or
family member first; the more practice, the better prepared you
are to deal with these types of people.

The Bully

Starting in childhood, we all have occasional run-ins with bullies. Their characteristics are quickly recognizable. You know the type—pushy, righteous, aggressive. They attempt to run over those around them with remarks such as "This is what we're doing—end of story" and "How could you be so stupid?"

You have several options in dealing with these human steamrollers:

1. Disagree without arguing.

Stay calm, don't argue, and practice assertive body language—uncross your arms, use direct eye contact. State the person's name at the beginning of your reply:

"John, I disagree."

"Mr. Adams, I see the situation differently."

"Terry, it's my understanding that... "

Don't say, "You're wrong on this," or "Who do you think you are?"

2. Solicit the person's point of view.

Show you're listening and want to understand:

"Mario, I see it differently. Help me understand why you think/feel this way."

"Ms. Francis, I have a different opinion. Perhaps you can give me an insight into the reasons you see it that way."

3. Take the initiative.

When dealing with bullies, take your turn to talk or they'll assume you agree. First, find some truth in what they have to say:

> "You're right, Ed, he did say that. Here's how I understood the comment... "

> "Mr. Genoa, what you said about time frame makes sense; however, I see that as a positive, not a negative."

Second, and just as important, don't allow interruptions:

> "Anya, I'm not finished. Thank you."

> "Mike, you interrupted me, I was saying... "

Don't say, "You never listen to me," or "I guess what I have to say doesn't matter."

The Smarty Pants

"Smarty pants" or "know-it-alls," for all their irritating behaviors, are often well meaning. They just give too much information, using facts and figures and an all-knowing attitude to confuse you and prove their point of view is the right one. Their communication style involves remarks such as: "Listen to me. I've been there before. It'll save you a lot of time if ... " or "What part don't you understand? One more time, read my lips—it's simple."

Just as with bullies, there's a simple set of strategies you can apply with "smarty pants":

1. **Feed back what they are saying, highlighting the main points.**

   As you'll remember from Chapter 4, this is one of the basics in responding assertively to feedback:

   "So, you're suggesting I skip the meeting and go straight to work on the project myself."

2. **Ask specific questions.**

   Asking questions not only elicits valuable information—it puts you in control of the interaction:

   "What is the due date on the project?"

   "How much time exactly are you talking about?"

   "Who will be at the meeting? Will Jim and Margaret stay for the entire presentation?"

3. **Thank them for their knowledge.**

   Recognition and acknowledgment are satisfying to a speaker, plus it softens up know-it-alls and may make them more inclined to listen to you:

   "Thanks for your input."

   "You've given me a lot to think about. I appreciate that."

The Back Stabber

Back stabbers have a lethal tongue that drips with innuendoes, sarcasm, and cruel humor that seeks its laugh at the expense of somebody else. These personalities never go head-to-head like the bully or the smarty pants; instead they whisper their attack under their breath or behind your back (often with you in earshot). They say things like "You got the promotion—I guess it pays to kiss up to the boss" and "That's a great idea! (under their breath) *For a moron.*"

The best way to deal with back stabbers is to turn the spotlight on them.

1. Call them on their remarks.

A useful tactic in diminishing the power of the back stabber is to respond swiftly and directly:

"Did you say something?"

"That sounded like a derogatory comment—did you mean it that way?"

2. Ask for their opinion.

Another means of neutralizing a back stabber's poisonous communications is to validate them as if they were legitimate opinions:

"I'm sure I heard you say something. I'm interested in your opinion."

"I sense you're not in agreement on this. What is it that's bothering you?"

"Why don't you tell me the problem so we can discuss it?"

3. Take a poll of the group.

When the back stabber performs in public, unmask the situation by soliciting the opinions (and thus also the attention) of others:

"How do the rest of you feel? Do you like the idea? Hate it? Let's open this up for discussion."

When you do this, make eye contact with an ally or neutral person; this takes the power away from the back stabber.

The Gloom and Doomer

Within the vital communications of the workplace, unchecked pessimists can take a real toll on creativity, productivity, and morale in general. You undoubtedly have encountered a "gloom and doomer"—someone who focuses consistently on what won't work, who denies the possibility of anything positive. Their negativity is a protection from disappointment when they say things like "It won't work, so why try?" or "But what if... "

Dealing with "the glass is half empty" types will require real energy from you, but the steps you can take are very straightforward:

1. Feed back, rephrase, or reflect their feelings.

You first need to isolate their basic concern or misgivings:

"So, if I understand you, you feel that it would be a waste of time."

"Let me see if I've grasped your concern here... "

2. Acknowledge some truth in what they say.

A reliable way of getting and holding the attention of pessimists is to validate their feedback:

"You're right, we have been somewhat unsuccessful with this in the past... "

"You may be correct that... "

"Just as you noted, the start-up costs will be high on this project... "

3. Be prepared to act on your own.

You may not often win over a "gloom and doomer" to your way of thinking or doing things, so make it clear when you're moving on, if that's what you've decided to do:

"I'm going ahead with the approval anyway."

"You've made some excellent points, and I'll never know for sure unless I try it myself."

"I'm willing to take that risk."

4. Solicit their help.

In some instances, it may be preferable to maintain a bridge with a negative person, or you may genuinely want that person's input even when you disagree on some key issues. When that's the case, don't hesitate to ask for the person's help:

"I know we're not in agreement on this, and while I'd like to have your support, I understand I may never get it. Still, I value your opinion and would gladly take any help you're willing to give."

"You made some very good points, and I'll definitely look into that before I leave. I know you'd like for me to reconsider, but I've decided to take the new position. I could really use your help during the transition. Would you be available to sit in on a meeting with my replacement?"

When You're the Difficult Person

Being emotional is not a curse; it means that you're a caring individual. How you handle your emotions, however, is critical to your credibility and assertiveness power. When you allow your emotions to get the best of you, it probably shows up in one of two disruptive ways: shouting and physical release (throwing objects or slamming doors), or tears. Both of these responses send a message of lack of control.

Two separate issues are at work here: first, how you avoid getting to the point of "losing it," and second, if you do "lose it" what you do then.

There are several steps you can take to steer away from losing control:

1. Take responsibility.

You're not a victim of your feelings. You can choose your response to the circumstances around you. The concept of responsibility is easy to grasp and yet not always easy to live. Continue to raise your self-awareness. Recognize that your emotions are a reflection of your thoughts and beliefs. Unless you're willing to take responsibility for your emotions, you are powerless over them.

When you feel yourself becoming emotional, ask yourself, "What is this about?" If it's about what someone has done to you, ask yourself, "If this had nothing to do with anyone but me, what would this be about?"

For example, you find out that you're being passed over for a promotion at work.

- What is this about?

  "I'm being cheated. This other person is getting my job, and they're only getting it because they go along with whatever the boss says."

- If this had nothing to do with anyone but me, what would it be about?

  "I'm disappointed. I'm afraid I'll never be good enough for a promotion. I'm angry at myself for not asking for the job."

Once you've identified your role in creating the emotion, you can evaluate it and take action.

2. Put things in perspective.

Ask yourself, "In the scope of life, how important is this?" The answer may be "not very." Perhaps you didn't really want the job—you just wanted to know you're an important person in the organization. If that's the case, the action that would make sense would be to discuss your contribution to the company with your boss and ask him or her for feedback.

On the other hand, this event may mean a great deal to you in the scope of life. In that case, ask yourself, "What actions can I take to forward myself?" If the goal is to get into management, use your assertiveness skills to find out what you need to do to make that happen. If the answer is not acceptable to you, it may be time to consider options outside of the company.

The point is this: Unless you evaluate what's causing the emotional explosion and take action to change things, you'll take the brunt of your emotions for the rest of your life.

3. If you're caught off guard, use an exit line.

Suppose you had no idea that a promotion was taking place until it's announced in a meeting of you and your peers. You feel the emotion building, and you know if you try to talk about it right now you're either going to burst out crying or throw your files against the wall. If you sense that you're not ready to have a rational discussion about something, the best thing to do is graciously excuse yourself.

Here are some effective exit lines:

> "You've given me a lot to think about. I would like to respond once I've had a chance to think this over (always set a time frame for resuming the discussion). How about if we continue this discussion after lunch?"

> "I can see you feel very strongly about this. Let's both think about it and talk again tomorrow. How does 9 o'clock sound?"

> "It doesn't seem like we're going to reach an agreement on this now. Let me consider what you've said, and I'll get back to you by the end of the day."

> "Would you excuse me for a minute? Thank you." (Use this only if you need a quick exit. Make sure that you return shortly once you're composed enough to use another of the exit lines.)

If, however, you are pushed to continue...

> "I understand the urgency here; that's why I'm suggesting we talk again before the end of the day. Thank you."

> "Rather than make an emotional decision, I am choosing to consider all that has been said before I respond. I appreciate your understanding. Thank you."

Although ideally you'll be able to head off an emotional reaction in one or more of the ways just described, sometimes it's too late—your emotions get the best of you and before you know it, you're in a full-swing tirade. Whether it's tears or physical anger, do the following:

- **Interrupt your behavior.**

  Take a deep breath and pause. Say to yourself, in your head, "Stop!"

- **State your feelings in a responsible manner.**

  When we report on our feelings, it often relieves the urge to act on them. Taking responsibility for them verbally will help you "save face" with your co-workers. For example:

  "As you can see, this is very important to me."

  "I am very frustrated and angry about what has happened."

  "If I look angry, it's because I am."

  Avoid saying anything like the following:

  "I'm not going to let you do this to me!"

  "You're right, I'm angry—wouldn't you be if this happened to you!"

  "This isn't fair!"

- **Continue or reschedule.**

  When tears get the best of you, if you're willing to continue and feel that you can, ask the other party involved if they'll continue the conversation. You may continue to cry. Crying is not the problem as much as how you handle it. If you're crying and choose to continue, *do not* apologize over and over, saying "I'm sorry, I can't believe I'm crying, I really didn't mean to." Instead, take a deep breath and ask whether the other person is okay with continuing. If the other person is distracted by your tears and would prefer to wait until you're less emotional, it's best to do so. In order to have an effective conversation, all parties must be present mentally, not focused on emotions.

If you want to continue, say something like: "As you can see, this is very important to me. I would like to continue if that is all right with you." And then wait for the response. Use your assertive communication skills as you continue. Take responsibility for your feelings, separate your assumptions and interpretations from the behavior and actions you are upset about, and maintain consistent eye contact.

If you're not comfortable continuing at that moment, ask to reschedule. Again, do not apologize for how you feel. Apologizing sends the message that "It's not okay for me to feel this way."

If you want to reschedule, say something on the order of this: "As you can see, I feel very strongly about this. I would like to continue this conversation a little later. How about (select a time)?" Once again, *do not apologize* for how you feel. If you deem it appropriate, you may apologize for any upset or discomfort your emotions may have caused: "I'm sorry if I have made you uncomfortable. This is a very important issue, and I do take it seriously. I appreciate your understanding."

If it's anger rather than tears that has you in its grip, make sure that you're willing and able to continue without physically displaying that you're upset. It's all right to be angry and even raise your voice, but throwing things and punching walls is not acceptable behavior and will definitely damage your credibility. In the case of physical anger, it's best to apologize for your actions—not how you feel—before continuing.

If you want to continue, say something like this: "I apologize for throwing the report on the ground; that wasn't appropriate behavior. This matter is very important, and I would like to discuss it now if you agree." (Wait for the response and honor it, whatever it is.)

If you feel it's best to continue at a later time, once again apologize for your actions if they were offensive and request a postponement, saying something on the order of the following: "Please forgive me for shouting at you; that wasn't necessary. This is extremely disappointing for me. I would like to discuss it further once I've had some time to think about it. Are you available at (request/specify a time)? Thank you."

Difficult people come with the territory, no matter what the profession or workplace. Although sometimes you may feel like you're performing in the Olympics of assertive communication in order to deal with them effectively, doing so will bolster your pride and self-confidence immeasurably and will win you the respect and loyalty of co-workers and supervisors alike.

Assert
Yourself!

Developing an assertive style is a process. Your willingness to take risks and try new ways of communicating will support you in becoming an assertive person.

When was the last time you embarked on an important journey of learning without feeling uncomfortable or awkward along the way? Chances are you will experience moments of fear and varying degrees of success when you first begin implementing the assertiveness skills discussed in this book. When you think about it, you probably had similar feelings when you learned how to ride a bike, but that didn't stop you from getting on the bike again and again until you could ride with "no hands" without even thinking about it.

So when you feel yourself getting "shaky," come back to this handbook for a refresher; tune in to your voice of possibility, brush yourself off, and "get back on the bike." You can count on YOU!

Bibliography
and Suggested
Resources

Alberti, Robert, and Michael Emmons. *Your Perfect Right.* San Luis Obispo, CA: Impact Publishers, 1990.

Brown Glase, Connie, and Barbara Steinberg Smalley. *More Power to You.* New York: Warner Books, 1992.

Carr-Ruffino, Norma. *The Promotable Woman.* Belmont, CA: Wadsworth Publishing, 1993.

Fleming, Carol. *The Sound of Your Voice.* New York: Simon and Schuster, 1988.

Garbor, Don. *Speaking Your Mind in 101 Difficult Situations.* New York: Simon and Schuster, 1994.

Heim, Pat. *Hardball For Women.* New York: Plume, 1992.

Helmster, Shad. *What To Say When You Talk to Yourself.* New York: Simon and Schuster, 1982.

Available From
SkillPath Publications

Self-Study Sourcebooks

Climbing the Corporate Ladder: What You Need to Know and Do to Be a Promotable Person *by Barbara Pachter and Marjorie Brody*

Coping With Supervisory Nightmares: 12 Common Nightmares of Leadership and What You Can Do About Them *by Michael and Deborah Singer Dobson*

Defeating Procrastination: 52 Fail-Safe Tips for Keeping Time on Your Side *by Marlene Caroselli, Ed.D.*

Discovering Your Purpose *by Ivy Haley*

Going for the Gold: Winning the Gold Medal for Financial Independence *by Lesley D. Bissett, CFP*

Having Something to Say When You Have to Say Something: The Art of Organizing Your Presentation *by Randy Horn*

Info-Flood: How to Swim in a Sea of Information Without Going Under *by Marlene Caroselli, Ed.D.*

The Innovative Secretary *by Marlene Caroselli, Ed.D.*

Letters & Memos: Just Like That! *by Dave Davies*

Mastering the Art of Communication: Your Keys to Developing a More Effective Personal Style *by Michelle Fairfield Poley*

Organized for Success! 95 Tips for Taking Control of Your Time, Your Space, and Your Life *by Nanci McGraw*

A Passion to Lead! How to Develop Your Natural Leadership Ability *by Michael Plumstead*

P.E.R.S.U.A.D.E.: Communication Strategies That Move People to Action *by Marlene Caroselli, Ed.D.*

Productivity Power: 250 Great Ideas for Being More Productive *by Jim Temme*

Promoting Yourself: 50 Ways to Increase Your Prestige, Power, and Paycheck *by Marlene Caroselli, Ed.D.*

Proof Positive: How to Find Errors Before They Embarrass You *by Karen L. Anderson*

Risk-Taking: 50 Ways to Turn Risks Into Rewards *by Marlene Caroselli, Ed.D. and David Harris*

Speak Up and Stand Out: How to Make Effective Presentations *by Nanci McGraw*

Stress Control: How You Can Find Relief From Life's Daily Stress *by Steve Bell*

The Technical Writer's Guide *by Robert McGraw*

Total Quality Customer Service: How to Make It Your Way of Life *by Jim Temme*

Write It Right! A Guide for Clear and Correct Writing *by Richard Andersen and Helene Hinis*

Your Total Communication Image *by Janet Signe Olson, Ph.D.*

Handbooks

The ABC's of Empowered Teams: Building Blocks for Success *by Mark Towers*

Assert Yourself! Developing Power-Packed Communication Skills to Make Your Points Clearly, Confidently, and Persuasively *by Lisa Contini*

Breaking the Ice: How to Improve Your On-the-Spot Communication Skills *by Deborah Shouse*

The Care and Keeping of Customers: A Treasury of Facts, Tips, and Proven Techniques for Keeping Your Customers Coming BACK! *by Roy Lantz*

Challenging Change: Five Steps for Dealing With Change *by Holly DeForest and Mary Steinberg*

Dynamic Delegation: A Manager's Guide for Active Empowerment *by Mark Towers*

Every Woman's Guide to Career Success *by Denise M. Dudley*

Grammar? No Problem! *by Dave Davies*

Great Openings and Closings: 28 Ways to Launch and Land Your Presentations With Punch, Power, and Pizazz *by Mari Pat Varga*

Hiring and Firing: What Every Manager Needs to Know *by Marlene Caroselli, Ed.D. with Laura Wyeth, Ms.Ed.*

How to Be a More Effective Group Communicator: Finding Your Role and Boosting Your Confidence in Group Situations *by Deborah Shouse*

How to Deal With Difficult People *by Paul Friedman*

Learning to Laugh at Work: The Power of Humor in the Workplace *by Robert McGraw*

Making Your Mark: How to Develop a Personal Marketing Plan for Becoming More Visible and More Appreciated at Work *by Deborah Shouse*

Meetings That Work *by Marlene Caroselli, Ed.D.*

The Mentoring Advantage: How to Help Your Career Soar to New Heights *by Pam Grout*

Minding Your Business Manners: Etiquette Tips for Presenting Yourself Professionally in Every Business Situation *by Marjorie Brody and Barbara Pachter*

Misspeller's Guide *by Joel and Ruth Schroeder*

Motivation in the Workplace: How to Motivate Workers to Peak Performance and Productivity *by Barbara Fielder*

NameTags Plus: Games You Can Play When People Don't Know What to Say *by Deborah Shouse*

Networking: How to Creatively Tap Your People Resources *by Colleen Clarke*

New & Improved! 25 Ways to Be More Creative and More Effective *by Pam Grout*

Power Write! A Practical Guide to Words That Work *by Helene Hinis*

The Power of Positivity: Eighty ways to energize your life *by Joel and Ruth Schroeder*

Putting Anger to Work For You *by Ruth and Joel Schroeder*

Reinventing Your Self: 28 Strategies for Coping With Change *by Mark Towers*

Saying "No" to Negativity: How to Manage Negativity in Yourself, Your Boss, and Your Co-Workers *by Zoie Kaye*

The Supervisor's Guide: The Everyday Guide to Coordinating People and Tasks *by Jerry Brown and Denise Dudley, Ph.D.*

Taking Charge: A Personal Guide to Managing Projects and Priorities *by Michal E. Feder*

Treasure Hunt: 10 Stepping Stones to a New and More Confident You! *by Pam Grout*

A Winning Attitude: How to Develop Your Most Important Asset! *by Michelle Fairfield Poley*

For more information, call 1-800-873-7545.

Notes

Notes